Clovis

Clovis

History of the Founder of Frank Monarchy

Collection

LM Publishers

Chapter 1[1]

In the third or fourth century (A.D.), there came paddling across the Rhine, in canoes and on rafts, bands of tall warriors, some of them with painted bodies and wild beasts' skins on their shoulders, others in gaudy woollen stuffs, some with iron breast-plates, many with gold chains round their necks, and all armed with either sword, axe, spear, mace, or pike. They were called Franks, and came from the forests of Germany, and the fens of the valley of the Danube. They were going to the country which was then called Gaul, and which after them was called France.

The Franks occupied the east bank of the Rhine for about two hundred years. Then many of the tribes

---

[1] Based on the work of John Bonner, in *The story history of France from the reign of Clovis, 481 A.D., to the signing of the armistice, November, 1918.*

crossed the river in search of new homes. The region west of the river was at that time called Gaul. Here the Franks established themselves and became a powerful people. (John H. Haaren)[2]

Gaul was at this time the home of a number of races which bore the names of Gauls, Celts, Beiges, Goths, Visigoths, Bretons, Iberians, and Burgundians, spoke the same or nearly the same language, and were brave, fierce, and rough. Among them was a sprinkling of Romans, and some of the young men of the native races had been educated at Rome, spoke Latin, wore clothes cut in the Roman fashion, and were mannered like the Romans. Some five hundred years before, the country had been conquered by the Romans under their valiant general, Julius Caesar, and had become a Roman province. It was for the most part a wild country, with much thicket, forest, marsh, swamp, and bare rock; cold fogs were frequent

---

[2] In *Famous Men of the Middle Ages.*

in the north; there were but few roads or bridges; to go from place to place travelers had to ride or trudge over bridle paths, through thick woods which were infested by wolves and bears, as well as by robbers and murderers. But on the plains and in the river valleys, especially in the south, were vineyards, orchards, and fields of waving grain; and in the towns, of which there were quite a number, stood theatres, circuses, aqueducts, churches, and temples. For the Romans improved every country they conquered.

They had had desperate work to conquer the Gauls.

Julius Caesar, the greatest general they ever had, spent nine whole years in fighting them. It looked as if they could not be conquered. The work was not done till Caesar had killed two millions of them, and till the rivers ran south to the Mediterranean and north to the British

Channel red with blood. Even the women fought like men, and died by their husbands' sides. There is a place in France which bears the dreadful name of Pourrieres ; if you go to see it, you will be told that a whole tribe men, women, and children were there butchered by the Roman soldiers, and their bodies left to rot in the sun.

At last, when the best fighting-men of every tribe had been killed, and the chiefs great, tall, splendid fellows, with blue eyes and tawny hair, and heads which towered above the Romans had been sent to Rome to march in Caesar's triumphal procession with their hands chained behind their backs, the Romans felt that Gaul was theirs.

The fighting was indeed over; the Gauls submitted to be ruled by Roman governors, and began in a feeble way to call themselves Romans.

It was a bad time to become a Roman. Soon after then, the great Roman Empire began to fall into ruin. It was crumbling to bits. Barbarians were swooping down on its borders and sacking its cities. Savages were bursting into its palaces and robbing them of their riches. Roman armies had lost their pluck, and instead of beating the enemy back gave him money and jewels to go away. Province after province was starting for itself, and declaring that it was not Roman any more. Meanwhile, whether the Empire lived or died, the gay people who lived at Rome went on leading luxurious lives, keeping hundreds of slaves to wait on them, eating food and drinking wine which were brought from distant countries, wearing beautiful clothes, spending millions of money, and taxing the submissive provinces to get it. One of the most submissive and the most grievously taxed was Gaul.

Every acre of land was taxed, every tree, every vine, every house and cow and pig and sheep, every barn and cart and plough; a man had to pay a tax for the wife he lived with, and a tax for every child she bore. Those who resisted the tax-gatherer were scourged with whips. The air echoed the groans and shrieks of women who were tortured to make them confess whether their husbands had property, and where it was hidden. After long endurance of this frightful oppression, the great heart of the Gauls broke. Caesar had taught them that they could not fight Rome. They just stopped tilling their fields and pruning their vines. They left their houses, fled into the woods where the cruel tax-gatherer could not reach them, and fell to robbing travelers and towns to feed their children. If this state of things had gone on, Gaul would have become a wilderness, the abode of wild beasts and men as wild as they.

It was then that the Franks came sailing across the Rhine into Gaul. They were a fighting people, hating work and loving war. They elected their king by vote: the strongest and bravest warrior was chosen, and was carried round on a shield on the arms of soldiers, who paraded him before the tribe. You will find in the histories of the Franks the names of several kings who are said to have led the Franks to battle: Pharamond, Clodion, Merovee, Childeric, and others. We know little about them and some historians don't feel sure that they were real personages. But there is no doubt of the reality of Clovis, or Chlodoveg as some of the old books call him. The people were very glad to see him all except the tax-gatherers. With these he had a short, sharp way of dealing. When a tax-gatherer got in his way, he sent one of his captains to argue with him;

and it was noticed that after the argument the tax-gatherer had nothing more to say. The Frank had persuaded him with his axe.

A few friends of Rome tried in a feeble way to oppose the march of the Franks, but Clovis persuaded them, too, with pike and sword; and the poor people came out of their hiding-places, and wrung the hands of the strangers, and bade them welcome. Nothing that Clovis could do to them could be worse than the oppression they had endured from the Romans. They made no objection when Clovis proclaimed himself master of town after town, valley after valley, province after province.

So, after a time, he came to rule over a larger country than any Gaulish chief had ever swayed and it was a country which, now that the people ventured to go to work once more on their farms, was worth governing. He called himself King of the Franks, but I think you had better emember him by the title which fits him best that of the First King of France.

Who really was Clovis?

Chapter 2

I

Clovis was born in the year 466. He succeeded his father as the King of the Franks of Tournai in 481.

Clovis was then only sixteen years of age. But though he was so young he proved in a very short time that he could govern as well as older men. He was intelligent and brave. No one ever knew him to be afraid of anything even when he was but a child. (John H. Haaren)

His kingdom was probably one of the States that sprang from the division of Clodion's monarchy like those of Cambrai, Tongres and Cologne. Although a Pagan, Childeric had kept up friendly relations with the bishops of Gaul, and when Clovis ascended the throne he received a most cordial letter of congratulation from St. Remigius, Archbishop of Reims. The young king early began his course of conquest by attacking Syagrius, son of Aegidius, the Roman Count.

Having established himself at Soissons, he acquired sovereign authority over so great a part of Northern Gaul as to be known to his contemporaries as the King of Soissons. Syagrius, being defeated, fled for protection to Alaric II, King of the Visigoths, but the latter, alarmed by a summons from Clovis, delivered Syagrius to his conqueror, who had him decapitated in 486.

When Clovis became king of the Franks a great part of Gaul still belonged to Rome. This part was then governed by a Roman general, named Syagrius. Clovis resolved to drive the Romans out of the country, and he talked over the matter with the head men of his army. "My desire," said he, "is that the Franks shall have possession of every part of this fair land. I shall drive the Romans and their friends away and make Gaul the empire of the Franks." (John H. Haaren)

II[3]

When Clovis succeeded his father as king of the Salians, the extent of his territory and the number of his subjects were, as we know, extremely small; at his death, he left to his successors a kingdom more extensive than that of modern France.

The influence of the grateful partiality discernible in the works of Catholic historians and chroniclers towards "the Eldest Son of the Church," who secured for them the victory over heathens on the one side, and heretics on the other, prevents us from looking to them for an unbiassed estimate of his character. Many of his crimes appeared to be committed in the cause of Catholicity itself, and these they could hardly see in their proper light. Pagans and Arians would have painted him in different colours;

---

[3] By Perry, W. Copland, in *The Franks, from their first appearance in history to the death of King Pepin.*

and had any of their works come down to us, we might have sought the truth between the positive of partiality and the negative of hatred. But fortunately, while the chroniclers praise his actions in the highest terms, they tell us what those actions were, and thus compel us to form a very different judgment from their own. It would not be easy to extract from the pages of his greatest admirers the slightest evidence of his possessing any qualities but those which are necessary to a conqueror. In the hands of Providence he was an instrument of the greatest good to the country he subdued, inasmuch as he freed it from the curse of division into petty states, and furthered the spread of Christianity in the very heart of Europe. But of any word or action that could make us admire or love the man, there is not a single trace in history. His undeniable courage is debased by a degree of cruelty unusual even in his times; and the consummate skill and prudence, which did more to raise him to his high position than even his military qualities, are rendered odious by the forms they take of unscrupulous falsehood, meanness, cunning and hypocrisy.

It will add to the perspicuity of our brief narrative of the conquests of Clovis, if we pause for a moment to consider the extent and situation of the different portions into which Gaul was divided at his accession.

There were in all six independent states:

1st, that of the Salians;

2nd, that of the Ripuarians;

3rd, that of the Visigoths;

4th, that of the Burgundians;

5th, the kingdom of Syagrius;

6th, Amorica (by which the whole sea-coast between Seine and Loire was then signified.)

The Visigoths held the whole of Southern Gaul. Their boundary to the north was the river Loire, and to the east the Pagus Vellavus (Auvergne). The boundary of the Burgundians on the side of Roman Gaul, was the Pagus Lingonicus (Upper Marne); to the west they were bounded by the territory of the Visigoths, as above described.

The territory still held by the Romans was divided into two parts, of which the one was held by Syagrius, who, according to common opinion, only ruled the country between Oise, Marne, and Seine; to this some writers have added Auxerre, Troyes, and Orleans. The other — *viz.*, that portion of Roman Gaul not subject to Syagrius — is of uncertain extent.

Armorica (Bretagne and Maine), was an independent state, inhabited by Britons and Saxons; but what was its form of government is not exactly known. It is important to bear these geographical divisions in mind, because they coincide with the successive Frankish conquests made under Clovis and his sons.

It would be unphilosophical to ascribe to Clovis a preconceived plan of making himself master of these several independent states, and of not only overthrowing the sole remaining pillar of the Roman Empire in Gaul, but, what was far more difficult, of subduing other German tribes, as fierce and independent, and in some cases more numerous than his own. In what he did, he was merely gratifying a passion for the excitements of war and acquisition, and that desire of expanding itself to its utmost limits, which is natural to every active, powerful, and imperious mind. He must indeed have been more than human to foresee, through all the obstacles that lay in his path, the career he was destined by Providence to run. He was not even master of the whole Salian tribe; and besides the Salians, there were other Franks on the Rhine, the Scheldt, the Meuse, and the Moselle, in no way inferior to his own subjects, and governed by kings of the same family as himself. Nor was Syagrius, to whom the anomalous power of his father Aegidius had descended, a despicable foe. His merits, indeed, were rather those of an able lawyer and a righteous judge than of a warrior; but he had acquired by his civil virtues a reputation which made him an object of envy to Clovis, who dreaded perhaps the permanent establishment of a Roman dynasty in Gaul. There were reasons for attacking Syagrius first, which can hardly have escaped the cunning of Clovis, and which doubtless guided him in the choice of his earliest victim. The very integrity of the noble

Roman's character was one of these reasons. Had Clovis commenced the work of destruction by attacking his kinsmen Sigebert of Cologne and Ragnachar of Cambrai, he would not only have received no aid from Syagrius in his unrighteous aggression, but might have found him ready to oppose it. But against Syagrius it was easy for Clovis to excite the national spirit of his brother Franks, both in and out of his own territory. In such an expedition, even had the kings declined to take an active part, he might reckon on crowds of volunteers from every Frankish *gau*.

As soon therefore as he had emerged from the forced inactivity of extreme youth (a period in which, fortunately for him, he was left undisturbed by his less grasping and unscrupulous neighbours), he determined to bring the question of pre eminence between the Franks and Romans to as early an issue as possible. Without waiting for a plausible ground of quarrel, he challenged Syagrius, more Germanico, to the field, that their respective fates might be determined by the God of Battles. Ragnachar of Cambrai was solicited to accompany his treacherous relative on this expedition, and agreed to do so. Chararich, another Frankish prince, whose alliance had been looked for, preferred waiting until fortune had decided, with the prudent intention of siding with the winner, and coming fresh into the field in time to spoil the vanquished.

Syagrius was at Soissons, which he had inherited from his father, when Clovis, with characteristic decision and rapidity, passed through the wood of Ardennes, and fell upon him with resistless force. The Roman was completely defeated, and the victor, having taken possession of Soissons, Rheims, and other Roman towns in the Belgica Secunda, extended his frontier to the river Loire, the boundary of the Visigoths. This battle took place in 486 (A.D.)

We know little or nothing of the materials of which the Roman army was composed. If it consisted entirely of Gauls, accustomed to depend on Roman aid, and destitute of the spirit of freemen, the ease with which Syagrius was defeated will cause us less surprise. Having lost all in a single battle, the unfortunate Roman fled for refuge to Toulouse, the court of Alaric, king of the Visigoths, who basely yielded him to the threats of the youthful conqueror.

But one fate awaited those who stood in the way of Clovis: Syagrius was immediately put to death, less in anger, than from the calculating policy which guided all the movements of the Salian's unfeeling heart.

During the next ten years after the death of Syagrius, there is less to relate of Clovis than might be expected from the commencement of his career.

We cannot suppose that such a spirit was really at rest: he was probably nursing his strength, and watching his opportunities; for, with all his impetuosity, he was not a man to engage in an undertaking without good assurance of success. Almost the only expedition of this inactive period of his life, is one recorded in a doubtful passage by Gregory of Tours, as having been made against the Tongrians. This people lived in the ancient country of the Eburones, on the Elbe, and had formerly been subjects of his mother Basina. The Tongrians were defeated, and their territory was, nominally at least, incorporated with the kingdom of Clovis.

In 493 (A.D.), he had married Clothildis, Chilperic the king of Burgundy's daughter, who, being herself a Christian, was naturally anxious to turn away her warlike spouse from the rude faith of his forefathers. The real result of her endeavours it is impossible to estimate, but, at all events, she has not received from history the credit of success. The mere suggestions of an affectionate wife would be considered as too simple and prosaic a means of accounting for a change involving such mighty consequences. The conversion of Clovis was so vitally important to the interests of the Catholic Church, that the chroniclers of that wonder-loving age, profuse in the employment of extraordinary means for the smallest ends, could never be brought to believe that this great event was the result of anything but a miracle of the most public and striking character.

Chapter 3 [4]

The baptism of Clovis, which implied the general conversion of the Franks to Christianity, set the crown on a century of striking successes for the Western Church. (Lewis Sergent)[5]

Four years had passed since the marriage of Clotilda and Clovis, and the latter was still a heathen. But the year 496 was not destined to pass until, according to the naive expression of the old Frankish chronicler, necessity had forced the king to confess that which, of his own free will, he had always denied.

Among the many wars which filled his reign the most noteworthy seems to have been that which he waged against the Alamanni. This Germanic people, established on the right bank

---

[4] Based on the work of Godefroid Kurth, in *Saint Clotilda*.

[5] In *The Franks - from their origin as a confederacy to the establishment of the kingdom of France and the German empire*.

of the Rhine, between the Maine and the Danube, was a worthy rival to the Frankish nation. They possessed all those great qualities which had won for the latter the sovereignty of Gaul, and they were quite competent to dispute its possession with some hope of success.

Moreover, their belligerent character and their need of expansion made it inevitable that they should break out into hostilities against their powerful neighbours.

It would seem to have been the Ripuarian Franks who first withstood the shock of the Alamannic bands. Beneath the walls of Tolbiac, at the entrance to the vast plain which formed the heart of the Ripuarian kingdom, the Alamanni, who had come down from the heights of the Eifel, came in contact with the army of King Sigebert, who lay in wait to intercept the road to Cologne. The battle was a bloody one, and Sigebert, who apparently remained master of the field, received a wound in his knee which made him lame for the rest of his life.

The danger to a nation who were the allies of the Salii and of a dynasty which was connected by marriage with his own, necessarily obliged Clovis to descend into the arena, apart from the fact that he probably had to defend his own frontiers against the inroads of his turbulent neighbours. In the dearth of all historical information, we can only indulge in conjectures concerning the causes of the war. All that we know for certain is that a great battle which promised to be decisive took place between the armies of the Franks and the Alamanni in the neighbourhood of the Rhine and probably in the direction of Alsace. According to the outcome of the battle, Gaul would have either remained in the possession of the Franks or have fallen as a long-coveted prey into the hands of their redoubtable foes. I may, perhaps, be allowed to transcribe from my Life of Clovis the account of this great crisis in Frankish history: — "Realising all that was at stake, Clovis had assembled his whole army, which was probably augmented by a contingent of Ripuarian Franks. On their side, the Alamanni must have had a no less considerable force drawn up in battle array, for they were not only able to hold the victory in suspense, but even at a given moment to drive back the Frankish regiments. The Alamannic furia was celebrated in battle; their warriors rushed to victory with an impetus that nothing could withstand. Brought face to face with their rivals, whose national pride had been excited by recent events, they knew they were playing for the highest stakes, and their realization of the gravity of the moment intensified their fever for the fight.

"Already they seemed to be within reach of victory. The Frankish army began to give way and a general rout seemed imminent. Clovis, who was fighting at the head of his troops, saw that the courage of his men was failing and that he could no longer bring them up to the assault. As in a flash of lightning there passed before his eyes all the horrors of defeat — all the disasters of flight. Then, on the point of perishing, abandoned by his Gods, whom he had invoked in vain, he seemed to hear once again, in his inner conscience, that much-loved voice that had spoken to him so often of a greater and more powerful God. And at the same moment, from the depths of his memory, stored with the words of Clotilda, there arose the figure of the loving and tender Christ, who was, as she had assured him, the vanquisher of death and the Prince of centuries to come. And in his despair he turned to Him with a cry of anguish and distress: 'Jesus Christ,' he exclaimed, according to the evidence of our ancient historian,' Thou who art, according to Clotilda, the Son of the living God, help me in my distress, and if Thou givest me victory, I will believe in Thee and will be baptized in Thy Name.'

"The words of Clovis have re-echoed through centuries and will be recorded by history through all time. Uttered in the midst of the horrors of the battle-field, from the depths of a royal heart speaking in the name of his people, they are something more than the words spoken by a man in a moment of peril; they represent the nation itself in the most solemn moment of its existence. Such is the historic import of the vow that fell from the lips of Clovis in that supreme moment: it was a pact proposed to Christ by the Frankish people, and which Christ ratified. For, writes the chronicler, scarcely had Clovis pronounced these words, when the fortunes of the field seemed suddenly to be reversed. As though they were conscious of the intervention of some new and powerful ally, the soldiers of Clovis recovered themselves; the Frankish troops returned to the charge, the Alamanni fell back in their turn, their king was killed in the melee, and the vanquishers saw themselves transformed into vanquished. The death of their leader gave a final blow to their valour; they flung away their arms, and on the very field of battle begged for mercy of the Frankish king. Clovis treated them with kindness and generosity, and, satisfied with the fact of their submission, he put an immediate end to the war."

Such, described from a contemporary source, is the history of the triumph of Clovis over the Alamanni, or rather, we may say, the triumph of Christianity over paganism. We find a worthy counterpart to this great battle in that of the Pons Milvius: the one closed the annals of the ancient world, the other opens the annals of the modern world. Its importance in history is therefore absolutely unique. Looking back from the point of vantage that fourteen centuries of time afford to the historian, we can perceive that the destinies of Europe were decided at the same time as those of the Frankish people, that the future of the Frankish people is to be traced to the victory of their king, and that all these mighty interests were dependent on the solution given, in the depths of a man's conscience, to the essential problem which presents itself to the soul of each one of us. It is here that lies the true interest of the event. The sudden action of a soul, which, arriving at a decision as in a flash of lightning, turned towards the Saviour of the world, displaced in a single instant the centre of gravity of history, gave birth to the first

Catholic nations, and placed in their hands the helm of civilization.

Nor must we forget that the triumph of Clovis was also the triumph of Clotilda. Her prayers and tears had at length prevailed, and the husband to whom she was deeply attached would never be taken from her, either in this world or the next. We will not attempt to describe her joy when she clasped the victor in her arms and learned the truth from his own lips. Moments of such pure and intense happiness are rare in any human life. For Clotilda it was the supreme moment of her existence, and its sweetness sufficed to radiate all her remaining years.

Later, sorrow engulfed her saintly soul and turned her days to a veritable martyrdom, but one joy could never be taken from her: that of having given to God the soul most dear to her on earth, and of having been chosen to unfold the Gospel to the greatest of Christian nations.

Clotilda was anxious that not a minute should be lost before securing the fruits of Clovis' vow.

Without delay she sent a message to St Remi, inviting him to Attigny, where, as seems probable, she was living for the time with her husband.

Secrecy was at first observed as regards the change that had come over the heart of the king, and meanwhile the work of his instruction was hurried forward. As a friend of the bishops, the husband of Clotilda, and the leader of a people a great number of whom were Catholics, Clovis was very far from being one of those untutored savages into whose heart no ray of Christianity had penetrated.

Nevertheless it is clear that the services of St Remi as a catechist were indispensable; he possessed a thorough knowledge of the barbarian world, he foresaw their brilliant future and, above all, he could claim the confidence of the king.

Before very long preparations were begun for the baptism of Clovis. But a question presented itself which was to be for some time a source of serious anxiety, both to the bishop and to the royal family.

It was not, as has been pointed out, among the Frankish people that any resistance to the king's conversion was likely to arise.

The barbarian Franks, scattered in times of peace among their Flemish and Brabantine farms, were in a state of complete ignorance as to what happened at court. Accustomed through long centuries to serve with fidelity the Christian Empire, whatever the religion of the chief who represented it might happen to be, they continued to live in all their heathen grossness without troubling themselves concerning the faith of other people. If their apathetic indifference left them in ignorance of Christian doctrines, at least they entertained towards them no feelings of disdain or of systematic hatred. They probably would have risen in revolt had the attempt been made to force

Christianity upon them, but the conversion of their king failed to excite in them the smallest indignation.

The sovereign did as he pleased, and they were his faithful warriors: such, in plain English, was the point of view of the vast majority of the Franks, and Clovis had no need to trouble himself about them.

It was quite another matter with the faithful bodyguard, which, bound to the king by a pledge of honour, was associated in all his acts and shared in his good and evil fortunes. The antrustions — for such was the name borne among the Franks by these chosen warriors — were closely linked to his daily life ; they shared in all his personal interests, in his friendships and enmities, and his Gods were their Gods.

What would become of this intimate communion of views and sentiments when Clovis passed from the service of Wodin to the service of Christ? It was absolutely essential that his antrustions should follow him to the foot of the new altars; otherwise the guard would disband itself, and the king, deprived of his glorious band of followers, would be stripped of all prestige.

But what guarantee had he that his faithful bodyguard would sacrifice their gods to their king?

Clovis was far from being entirely at ease on this point. "I am ready to listen to you," he assured St Remi, "but my followers will not forsake their gods." These words, which the chronicler attributes to him, sum up with great precision the problem which the powerful monarch had to face. As there was no possibility of taking any definite steps until he had arrived at some understanding with the antrustions, Clovis summoned them to a meeting, explained his intentions and asked their advice. As with one voice, they all declared that they were ready to forsake their mortal gods, and to accept the eternal God announced to them by Clovis.

Thus, by a readiness which the Frankish chronicler accepts as providential, they disposed of the one serious obstacle that existed to the conversion of Clovis. There only remained to fix the date of the event.

"An ancient tradition which was said to have come down from apostolic times, ordained that the sacrament of baptism should only be administered on Easter Sunday in order that this great festival might be, in a sense, a day of resurrection both for God and for men. But, in the opinion of the bishops, a respect for tradition should not be allowed to override the very important reasons that existed for not prolonging the catechumenate of the king and his followers. Taking into consideration the unique circumstances of the case, it was deemed advisable to make an exception to the ordinary rule, and to fix the ceremony for Christmas Day. After the Easter festival the Nativity was undoubtedly the feast which by its mystical significance, and by the imposing solemnity of its rites, best lent itself to the great event that was about to take place.

"Clovis arranged with the bishops that the feast should be celebrated with all possible magnificence. All the most important personages of his realm were invited to be present, and invitations were issued moreover to princes of the Church beyond the frontiers of the kingdom. We know at least by a letter from St Avitus of Vienne that the illustrious prelate was among those bidden to be present. The baptism of Clovis took on itself the importance of an international event. Christian Gaul followed the preparations with a sympathetic interest; the princes of the Catholic hierarchy turned their eyes full of hope towards the Frankish nation, and a tremor of joy passed through the Church which in so many lands was languishing under the yoke of heresy.

"The great day dawned at last which was to convert the Frankish nation into the eldest daughter of the Catholic Church. It was the

25th of December 496. Never since its first foundation had the city of Reims been witness of so imposing a solemnity; nor had it been behindhand in displaying all the pomp necessary for its worthy celebration.

Rich carpets adorned the fronts of the houses; great embroidered veils, stretched across the streets, cast solemn shadows; the churches were radiant in all their finery, the baptistery was adorned with almost inconceivable grandeur, and countless candles shone through the clouds of ascending incense. There was something celestial in the sweet odour, writes the old chronicler, and those who, by the grace of God, were witnesses of the ceremony, might have imagined themselves transplanted into the midst of the joys of Paradise.

"From the ancient palace of the Governors of Lower Belgium, where he had taken up his residence, the Frankish king, followed by a triumphal procession, made his way amid the enthusiastic acclamations of the crowd to the Cathedral of Notre Dame, where the baptism was to take place. 'He advanced,' writes a contemporary author, 'like a second Constantine to the baptismal font to be cleansed from the leprosy of sin, and the stains of former guilt were about to be washed away in the laver of regeneration.' The procession was formed in accordance with the ecclesiastical ritual. At its head was carried a cross, followed by the sacred books borne by clerics ; then came the king led by the bishop, as though to guide him into the House of God. Behind them walked Clotilda, the true heroine of the day, and she was accompanied by the youthful Theodoric, who was to follow his father to the font, and by the Princesses Lanthilda and Albofleda, the former an Arian, and the latter still plunged in the darkness of heathenism. Three thousand Franks, among whom were all the king's bodyguard, followed their sovereign, and came, like him, to acknowledge the God of Clotilda as the supreme power. The Litany of the Saints alternated with the Church's most triumphant hymns, and re-echoed through the festive town, like chants in the celestial kingdom. 'Is this,' asked Clovis of St Remi, 'the kingdom of heaven that you promised me?' 'No,' answered the prelate, ' but it is the beginning of the road that leads thither.' Arrived at the threshold of the baptistery, where the bishops who were to take part in the ceremony came to meet the procession, it was the king who spoke first and requested St Remi to confer upon him the Sacrament of Baptism. It is well, great Sicamber,' answered the priest; ' bow down thy neck with meekness, adore what thou hast hitherto burned and burn what thou hast adored.' And forthwith the sacred ceremony commenced, with all the solemnity that has been observed through long centuries. Replying to the liturgical questions of the officiating priest, the king declared that he renounced the worship of Satan, and repeated his profession of the Catholic faith in which, in accordance with the special needs of a time in which Arianism was rampant, the belief in the Most Holy Trinity was formulated with extreme precision.

Then, stepping down into the baptismal waters, he received the triple sacramental immersion in the name of the Father, and of the Son, and of the Holy Ghost.

On leaving the baptistery he received further the Sacrament of Confirmation, in accordance with the custom observed at adult baptisms. The members of the royal family were immersed after the king. Lanthilda, who was already a Christian, was not re-baptized, but merely received confirmation according to the Catholic rite. As regards the three thousand Franks who crowded round the sacred edifice, it is probable that they were baptized by aspersion, which was already practiced at that date. All the newly baptized were subsequently clothed in white garments, typical of the state of grace into which they had entered in virtue of the Sacrament of Regeneration."

One circumstance will have impressed the reader in this description, the main points of which have been taken from the most ancient sources: we refer to the presence of Clotilda in the baptismal procession. It was her work which received its final crown on this day of festivity. Who, better than she, deserved to rejoice and to be a happy witness of the event? Like that other valiant Christian, Joan of Arc, who, a thousand years later, was to lead the triumphal procession of another king to that same Church, she had borne the heat of the day and it was only just that she should have her share of honour.

Chapter 4 [6]

The sincerity of Clovis's conversion has been called in question for many reasons, — such as the unsuitability of his subsequent life to Christian principles, — but chiefly on the ground of the many political advantages to be derived from a public profession of the Catholic Faith. We are too ready with such explanations of the actions of distinguished characters, too apt to forget that politicians are also men, and to overlook the very powerful influences which lie nearer to their hearts than even political calculation. A spirit was abroad in the world, drawing men away from the graves of a dead faith to the life and light of the Gospel, — a spirit which not even the coldest and sternest heart could altogether resist. There was

---

[6] This chapter and the following are based on the work of Perry, W. Copland.

something, too, peculiarly imposing in the attitude of the Christian Church at that period. All else in the Roman world seemed dying of mere weakness and old age — the Christian Church was still in the vigour of youth, and its professors were animated by indomitable perseverance and boundless zeal. All else fell down in terror before the Barbarian conqueror — the fabric of the Church seemed indestructible, and its ministers stood erect in his presence, as if depending for strength and aid upon a power, which was the more terrible, because indefinite in its nature and uncertain in its mode of operation.

Nor were there wanting to the Catholic Church, even at that stage of its development, those external neans of influence which tell with peculiar force upon the barbarous and untutored mind. The emperors of the Roman world had reared its temples, adorned its shrines, and regulated its services, in a manner which seemed to them best suited to the majesty of Heaven and their own. Its altars were served by men distinguished by their learning, and by that indestructible dignity of deportment, which is derived from conscious superiority. The praises of God were chaunted forth in well-chosen words and impressive tones, or sung in lofty strains by tutored voices; while incense rose to the vaulted aisle, as if to bear the prayers of the kneeling multitude to the very gates of Paradise.

And Clovis was as likely to be worked upon by such means as the meanest of his followers. We must not suppose that the discrepancy between his Christian profession and his public and private actions, which we discern so clearly, was equally evident to himself. How should it be so? His own conscience was not especially enlightened beyond the measure of his age. The bravest warriors of his nation hailed him as a patriot and hero, and the ministers of God assured him that his victories were won in the service of Truth and Heaven. It is always dangerous to judge of the sincerity of men's religious — perhaps we should say theological — convictions by the tenor of their moral conduct, and this even in our own age and nation; but far more so in respect to men of other times and countries, at a different stage of civilization and religious development, at which the scale of morality was not only lower, but differently graduated from our own.

The conscience of a Clovis remained undisturbed in the midst of deeds whose enormity makes us shudder; and, on the other hand, how trivial in our eyes are some of those offences which loaded him with the heaviest sense of guilt! The eternal laws of the God of justice and mercy might be broken with impunity; and what we should call the basest treachery and the most odious cruelty, employed to compass the destruction of an heretical or pagan enemy; but woe to him who offended St. Martin, or laid a finger on the property of the meanest of his servants ! When Clovis was seeking to gratify his lust of power, he believed, no doubt, that he was at the same time fighting under the banner of Christ, and destroying the enemies of God. And no wonder, for many a priest and bishop thought the same, and told him what they thought.

We are, however, far from affirming that the political advantages to be gained from an open avowal of the Catholic Faith at this juncture escaped the notice of so astute a mind as that of Clovis. No one was more sensible of those advantages than he was.

The immediate consequences were indeed apparently disastrous. He was himself fearful of the effect which his change of religion might have upon his Franks, and we are told that many of them left him and joined his kinsman Ragnarich. But the ill effects, though immediate, were slight and transient, while the good results went on accumulating from year to year. In the first place, his baptism into the Catholic Church conciliated for him the zealous affection of his Gallo-Roman subjects, whose number and wealth, and, above all, whose superior knowledge and intelligence, rendered their aid of the utmost value.

With respect to his own Franks, we are justified in supposing that, removed as they were from the sacred localities with which their faith was intimately connected, they either viewed the change with indifference, or, wavering between old associations and present influences, needed only the example of the king to decide their choice, and induce them to enlist under the banner of the Cross.

The German neighbours of Clovis had either preserved their ancient faith or adopted the Arian heresy. His conversion therefore was advantageous or disadvantageous to him, as regarded them, according to the objects he had in view. Had he really desired to live with his compatriot kings on terms of equality and friendship, his reception into a hostile Church would certainly not have furthered his views. But nothing was more foreign to his thoughts than friendship and alliance with any of the neighbouring tribes. His desire was to reduce them all to a state of subjection to himself. He had the genuine spirit of the conqueror, which cannot brook the sight of independence; and his keen intellect and unflinching boldness enabled him to see his advantages and to turn them to the best account.

Even in those countries in which Heathenism or Arian Christianity prevailed, there was generally a zealous and united community of Catholic Christians (including all the Romance inhabitants), who, being outnumbered and sometimes persecuted, were inclined to look for aid abroad. Clovis became by his conversion the object of hope and attachment to such a party in almost every country on the continent of Europe. He had the powerful support of the whole body of the Catholic clergy, in whose hearts the interests of their Church far outweighed all other considerations. In other times and lands (in our own for instance) the spirit of loyalty and the love of country have often sufficed to counteract the influence of theological opinions, and have made men patriots in the hour of trial, when their spiritual allegiance to an alien head tempted them to be traitors. But what patriotism could Gallo-Romans feel, who for ages had been the slaves of slaves? or what loyalty to barbarian oppressors, whom they despised as well as feared ?

The happy effects of Clovis's conversion were not long in showing themselves. In the very next year after that event (497 A.D.) the Armoricans, inhabiting the country between the Seine and Loire, who had stoutly defended themselves against the heathen Franks, submitted with the utmost readiness to the royal convert,whom bishops delighted to honour; and in almost every succeeding struggle the advantages he derived from the strenuous support of the Catholic party become more and more clearly evident.

Chapter 5

In 500 (A.D.) Clovis reduced the Burgundians to a state of semi-dependence, after a fierce and bloody battle with Gundobald, their king, at Dijon on the Ousche. In this conflict, as in almost every other, Clovis attained his ends in a great measure by turning to account the dissensions of his enemies. Gundobald had called upon his brother Godegisil, who ruled over one division of their tribe, to aid him in repelling the attack of the Franks. The call was answered, in appearance at least; but in the decisive struggle Godegisil, according to a secret understanding, deserted with all his forces to the enemy. Gundobald was of course defeated, and submitted to conditions which, however galling to his pride and patriotism, could not have been very severe, since we find him immediately afterwards punishing the treachery of his brother, whom he besieged in the city of Vienne, and put to death in an Arian Church.

The circumstances of the times, rather than the moderation of Clovis, prevented him from calling Gundobald to account. A far more arduous struggle was at hand, which needed all the wily Salian's resources of power and policy to bring to a successful issue — the struggle with the powerful king and people of the Visigoths, whose immediate neighbour he had become after the voluntary submission of the Armoricans in 497 (A.D.). The valour and conduct of their renowned king Euric had put the Western Goths in full possession of all that portion of Gaul which lay between the rivers Loire and Rhone, together with nearly the whole of Spain. That distinguished monarch had lately been succeeded by his son Alaric II., who was now in the flower of youth. It was in the war with this ill-starred prince — the most difficult and doubtful in which he had been engaged — that Clovis experienced the full advantages of his recent change of faith. King Euric, who was an Arian, wise and great as he appears to have been in many respects, had alienated the affections of multitudes of his people by persecuting the Catholic minority x ; and though the same charge does not appear to lie against Alaric, it is evident that the hearts of his orthodox subjects beat with no true allegiance towards their heretical king. The baptism of Clovis had turned their eyes towards him, as one who would not only free them from the persecution of their theological enemies, but procure for them and their Church a speedy victory and a secure predominance. The hopes they had formed, and the aid they were ready to afford him, were not unknown to Clovis, whose eager rapacity was only checked by the consideration of the part which his brother-in-law Theoderic, King of the Ostrogoths, was likely to take in the matter. This great and enlightened Goth, whose refined magnificence renders the contemptuous sense in which we use the term Gothic more than usually inappropriate, was ever ready to mediate between kindred tribes of Germans, whom on every suitable occasion he exhorted to live in unity, mindful of their common origin. He is said on this occasion to have brought about a meeting between Clovis and Alaric on a small island in the Loire in the neighbourhood of Amboise. The story is very doubtful, to say the least. Had he done so much, he would probably have done more, and have shielded his youthful kinsman with his strong right arm.

Whatever he did was done in vain. The Frankish conqueror knew his own advantages and determined to use them to the utmost. He received the aid not only of his kinsman Sigebert of Cologne, who sent an army to his support under Chararich, but of the king of the Burgundians, who was also a Catholic. With an army thus united by a common faith, inspired by religious zeal, and no less so by the Frankish love of booty, Clovis marched to almost certain victory over an inexperienced leader and a kingdom divided against itself.

It is evident, from the language of Gregory of Tours, that this conflict between the Franks and

Visigoths was regarded by the orthodox party of his own and preceding ages as a religious war, on which, humanly speaking, the prevalence of the Catholic or the Arian creed in Western Europe depended.

Clovis did everything in his power to deepen this impression. He could not, he said, endure the thought that "those Arians" held a part of his beautiful Gaul. 1 As he passed through the territory of Tours, which was supposed to be under the peculiar protection of St. Martin, he was careful to preserve the strictest discipline among his soldiers, that he might further conciliate the Church and sanctify his undertaking.

On his arrival at the city of Tours, he publicly displayed his reverence for the patron saint, and received the thanks and good wishes of a whole chorus of priests assembled in St. Martin's Church. He was guided (according to one of the legends by which his progress has been so profusely adorned) through the swollen waters of the river Vienne by "a hind of wonderful magnitude;" and, as he approached the city of Poitiers, a pillar of fire (whose origin we may trace, as suits our views, to the favour of heaven or the treachery of man) shone forth from the cathedral, to give him the assurance of success, and to throw light upon his nocturnal march. The Catholic bishops in the kingdom of Alaric were universally favourable to the cause of Clovis, and several of them, who had not the patience to postpone the manifestation of their sympathies, were expelled by Alaric from their sees. The majority indeed made a virtue of necessity, and prayed continually and loudly, if not sincerely, for their lawful monarch. Perhaps they had even in that age learned to appreciate the efficacy of mental reservation.

Conscious of his own weakness, Alaric retired before his terrible and implacable foe, in the vain hope of receiving assistance from the Ostrogoths. He halted at last in the plains of Vouglé, behind Poitiers, but even then rather in compliance with the wishes of his soldiers than from his own deliberate judgment. His soldiers, drawn from a generation as yet unacquainted with war, and full of that overweening confidence which results from inexperience, were eager to meet the enemy. Treachery, also, was at work to prevent him from adopting the only means of safety, which lay in deferring as long as possible the too unequal contest. The Franks came on with their usual impetuosity, and with a well-founded confidence in their own prowess; and the issue of the battle was in accordance with the auspices on either side. Clovis, no less strenuous in actual fight than wise and cunning in council, exposed himself to every danger, and fought hand to hand with Alaric himself. Yet the latter was not slain in the field, but in the disorderly flight into which the Goths were quickly driven.

The victorious Franks pursued them as far as Bordeaux, where Clovis passed the winter, while Theocleric, his son, was overrunning Auvergne, Quincy, and Rovergne. The Goths, whose new king was a minor, made no further resistance; and in the following year the Salian chief took possession of the royal treasure at Toulouse. He also took the town of Angouleme, at the capture of which he was doubly rewarded for his services to the Church, for not only did the inhabitants of that place rise in his favour against the Visigothic garrison, but the very walls, like those of Jericho, fell down at his approach!

In 508 (A.D.), a short time after these events, Clovis received the titles and dignity of Roman Patricius and Consul from the Greek Emperor Anastasius; who appears to have been prompted to this act more by motives of jealousy and hatred towards Theoderic the Ostrogoth, than by any love he bore the restless and encroaching Frank. The meaning of these obsolete titles, as applied to those who stood in no direct relation to either division of the

Roman Empire, has never been sufficiently explained. We are at first surprised that successful warriors and powerful kings like Clovis, Pepin, and Charlemagne himself, should condescend to accept such empty honours at the hands of the miserable eunuch-ridden monarchs of the East. That the Byzantine Emperors should affect a superiority over contemporary sovereigns is intelligible enough; the weakest idiot among them, who lived at the mercy of his women and his slaves, had never resigned one title of his pretensions to that universal empire which an Augustus and a Trajan once possessed. But whence the acquiescence of Clovis and his great successors in this arrogant assumption? We may best account for it by remarking how long the prestige of power survives the strength that gave it. The sun of Rome was set, but the twilight of her greatness still rested on the world. The German kings and warriors received with pleasure, and wore with pride, a title which brought them into connection with that imperial city, of whose universal dominion, of whose skill in arms and arts, the traces lay everywhere around them.

Nor was it without some solid advantages in the circumstances in which Clovis was placed. He ruled over a vast population, which had not long ceased to be subjects of the Empire, and still rejoiced in the Roman name. He fully appreciated their intellectual superiority, and had already experienced the value of their assistance. Whatever, therefore, tended to increase his personal dignity in their eyes (and no doubt the solemn proclamation of his Roman titles had this tendency) was rightly deemed by him of no small importance.

In the same year that he was invested with the diadem and purple robe in the church of St.

Martin at Tours the encroaching Franks had the southern and eastern limits of their kingdom marked out for them by the powerful hand of Theoderic the Great. The brave but peace-loving Goth had trusted too much to his influence with Clovis, and had hoped to the last to save the unhappy Alaric, by warning and mediation. The slaughter of the Visigoths, the death of Alaric himself, the fall of Angouleme and Toulouse, the advance of the Franks upon the Rhone, where they were now besieging Aries, had effectually undeceived him. He now prepared to bring forward the only arguments to which the ear of a Clovis is ever open, — the battle-cry of a superior army. His faithful Ostrogoths were summoned to meet in the month of June,

508 (A.D.), and he placed a powerful army under the command of Eva (Ibba or Hebba), who led his forces into Gaul over the southern

Alps. The Franks and Burgundians, who were investing Aries and Carcassonne, raised the siege and retired, but whether without or in consequence of a battle, is rendered doubtful by the conflicting testimony of the annalists. The subsequent territorial position of the combatants, however, favours the account that a battle did take place, in which Clovis and his allies received a most decided and bloody defeat.

The check thus given to the extension of his kingdom at the expense of other German nations, and the desire perhaps of collecting fresh strength for a more successful struggle hereafter, seem to have induced Clovis to turn his attention to the destruction of his Merovingian kindred. The manner in which he effected his purpose is related with a fullness which naturally excites suspicion. But though it is easy to detect both absurdity and inconsistency in many of the romantic details with which Gregory has furnished us, Ave see no reason to deny to his statements a foundation of historical truth.

Clovis was still but one of several Frankish kings; and of these Sigebert of Cologne, king of the Ripuarians, was little inferior to him in the extent of his dominions and the number of his subjects. But in other respects — in mental activity and bodily prowess — "the lame" Sigebert was no match for his Salian brother.

The other Frankish rulers were, Chararich, of whom mention has been made in connection

with Syagrius, and Ragnachar (or Ragnachas), who held his court at Cambrai. The kingdom of Sigebert extended along both banks of the Rhine, from Mayence down to Cologne; to the west along the Moselle as far as

Treves; and on the east to the river Fulda and the borders of Thuringia. The Franks who occupied this country are supposed to have taken possession of it in the reign of Valentinian III., when Mayence, Cologne, and Treves, were conquered by a host of Ripuarians. Sigebert, as we have seen, had come to the aid of Clovis, in two very important battles with the Alemanni and the Visigoths, and had shown himself a ready and faithful friend whenever his co-operation was required. But gratitude was not included among the graces of the champion of Catholicity, who only waited for a suitable opportunity to deprive his ally of throne and life.

The present juncture was favourable to his wishes, and enabled him to rid himself of his benefactor in a manner peculiarly suited to his taste. An attempt to conquer the kingdom of Cologne by force of arms would have been but feebly seconded by his own subjects, and would have met with a stout resistance from the Ripuarians, who were conscious of no inferiority to the Salian tribe. His efforts were therefore directed to the destruction of the royal house, the downfall of which was hastened by internal divisions. Clotaire (or Clotarich), the expectant heir of Sigebert, weary of hope deferred, gave a ready ear to the hellish suggestions of Clovis, who urged him, by the strongest appeals to his ambition and cupidity, to the murder of his father.

Sigebert was slain by his own son in the Buchonian Forest near Fulda. The wretched parricide endeavoured to secure the further connivance of his tempter, by offering him a share of the blood-stained treasure he had acquired. But Clovis, whose part in the transaction was probably unknown, affected a feeling of horror at the unnatural crime, and procured the immediate assassination of Clotaire; an act which rid him of a rival, silenced an embarrassing accomplice, and tended rather to raise than to lower him in the opinion of the Ripuarians.

It is not surprising, therefore, that when Clovis proposed himself as the successor of Sigebert, and promised the full recognition of all existing rights, his offer should be joyfully accepted.

In 509 (A.D.) he was elected king by the Ripuarians, and raised upon a shield in the city of Cologne, according to the Frankish custom, amid general acclamation.

"And thus, said Gregory of Tours, " God daily prostrated his enemies before him and increased his kingdom, because he walked before him with an upright heart, and did what was pleasing in his eyes!" — so completely did his services to the Catholic Church conceal his moral deformities from the eyes of even the best of the ecclesiastical historians.

To the destruction of his next victim, Chararich, whose power was far less formidable than that of Sigebert, he was impelled by vengeance as well as ambition. That cautious prince, instead of joining the other Franks in their attack upon Syagrius, had stood aloof and waited upon fortune. Yet we can hardly attribute the conduct of Clovis towards him chiefly to revenge, for his most faithful ally had been his earliest victim; and friend and foe were alike to him, if they did but cross the path of his ambition.

After getting possession of Chararich and his son, by tampering with their followers, Clovis compelled them to cut off their royal locks and become priests; subsequently, however, he caused them to be put to death.

Ragnachar of Cambrai, whose kingdom lay to the north of the Somme, and extended through Flanders and Artois, might have proved a more formidable antagonist, had he not become unpopular among his own subjects by the disgusting licentiousness of his manners.

The account which Gregory gives of the manner in which his ruin was effected is more curious than credible, and adds the charge of swindling to the black list of crimes recorded against the man who "walked before God with an upright heart." According to the historian, Clovis bribed the followers of Ragnachar with armour of gilded iron, which they mistook, as he intended they should, for gold.

Having thus crippled by treachery the strength of his enemy, Clovis led an army over the Somme, for the purpose of attacking him in his own territory.

Ragnachar prepared to meet him, but was betrayed by his own soldiers and delivered into the hands of the invader. Clovis, with facetious cruelty, reproached the fallen monarch for having disgraced their common family by suffering himself to be bound, and then split his skull with an axe. The same absurd charge was brought against Kichar, the brother of Ragnachar, and the same punishment inflicted on him. A third brother was put to death at Mans.

Gregory refers, though not by name, to other kings of the same family, who were all destroyed by Clovis. "Having killed many other kings," he says, "who were his kinsmen, because he feared they might deprive him of his power, he extended his kingdom through the whole of Gaul." He also tells us that the royal hypocrite, having summoned a general assembly, complained before it, with tears in his eyes, that he was "alone in the world." "Alas, for me!" he said, "I am left as an alien among strangers, and have no relations who can assist me." This he did, according to Gregory, "not from any real love of his kindred, or from remorse at the thought of his crimes, but that he might find out any more relations and put them also to death."

Clovis died at Paris, 27 November, 511 (A.D.), in the forty-fifth year of his age and the thirtieth of his active, blood-stained, and eventful reign. He lived therefore only five years after the decisive battle of Vouglé.

Chapter 6

It would derogate from our opinion of the political sagacity of Clovis, were we to attribute to his personal wishes the partition of his kingdom among his four sons. We have no account, moreover, of any testamentary dispositions made by him to this effect, and are justified in concluding that the division took place in accordance with the general laws of inheritance which then prevailed among the Germans.

However clearly he may have foreseen the disastrous consequences of destroying the unity which it had been one object of his life to effect, his posthumous influence would hardly have sufficed to reconcile his younger sons to their own exclusion, supported as they would naturally be by the national sympathy in the unusual hardship of their lot.

Of the four sons of Clovis, Theoderic (Dietrich, Thierry), Clodomir, Childebert, and Clotar (Clotaire), the eldest, who was then probably about twenty-four years of age, was the son of an unknown mother, and the rest, the offspring of the Burgundian princess Clothildis. The first use they made of the royal power which had descended to them was to divide the empire into four parts; in which division, though Gregory describes them as sharing " *aequa lance*," the eldest son appears to have had the lion's share.

We should in vain endeavour to understand the principles on which this partition was made, and it is no easy matter to mark the limits of the several kingdoms. Theoderic, King of Austrasia (or Metz), for example, obtained the whole of the Frankish territories which bordered on the Rhine, and also some provinces in the south of

Gaul. His capital cities were Metz and Itheims, from the former of which his kingdom took its name. Clodomir had his residence at Orleans, Childebert at Paris, and Clotaire at Soissons; and these three cities were considered as the capitals of the three divisions of the empire over which they ruled.

The exact position and limits of their respective territories cannot be defined with any certainty, but we may fairly surmise, from the position of the towns above mentioned, that the middle part of Neustria belonged to the kingdom of Paris, the southern part to Orleans, and the north-eastern to Soissons.

The kingdom of Theoderic, as will be seen by a reference to the map, corresponded in a great measure with the region subsequently called Austrasia (Eastern Land) in contradistinction to Neustria, which included the more recently acquired possessions of the Franks. These terms are so frequently used in the subsequent history, and the distinction they denote was so strongly marked and has been so permanent, that an explanation of them cannot but be useful to the reader.

It is conjectured by Luden, with great probability, that the Ripuarians were originally called the Eastern people to distinguish them from the Salian Franks who lived to the west. But when the old home of the conquerors on the right bank of the Rhine was united with their new settlements in Gaul, the latter, as it would seem, were called Neustria or Neustrasia (New Lands); while the term Austrasia came to denote the original seats of the Franks, on what we now call the German bank of the Rhine. The most important difference between them (a difference so great as to lead to their permanent separation into the kingdoms of France and

Germany by the treaty of Verdun) was this, that in Neustria the Frankish element was quickly absorbed by the mass of Gallo-Romanism by which it was surrounded; while in Austrasia, which included the ancient seats of the Frankish conquerors, the German element was wholly predominant.

The import of the word Austrasia (Austria, Austrifrancia) is very fluctuating. In its widest sense it was used to denote all the countries incorporated into the Frankish Empire, or even held in subjection to it, in which the German language and population prevailed; in this acceptation it included therefore the territory of the Alemanni, Bavarians, Thuringians, and even that of the Saxons and Frises. In its more common and proper sense it meant that part of the territory of the Franks themselves which was not included in Neustria. It was subdivided into Upper Austrasia on the Moselle, and Lower Austrasia on the Rhine and Meuse.

Neustria (or, in the fulness of the Monkish Latinity, Neustrasia) was bounded on the north by the ocean, on the south by the Loire, and on the south-west towards Burgundy by a line which, beginning below Gien on the Loire, ran through the rivers Loing and Yonne, not far from their sources, and passing north of Auxerre and south of Troyes, joined the river Aube above Arcis. The western boundary line again by which Neustria was separated from Austrasia, commencing at the river Aube, crossed the Marne to the east of Chateau Thierry, and passing through the rivers Aisne and Oise, and round the sources of the Somme, left Cambrai on the east, and reached the Scheldt, which it followed to its mouth.

The tide of conquest had not reached its height at the death of Clovis. Even in that marauding age the Franks were conspicuous among the German races for their love of warlike adventure; and the union of all their different tribes under one martial leader, who kept them almost perpetually in the field, gave them a strength which none of their neighbours were able to resist. The partition of the kingdom afforded indeed a favourable opportunity to the semi-dependent states of throwing off the yoke which Clovis had imposed; but neither the Burgundians nor the Visigoths were in a condition to make the attempt, and Theoderic, the powerful king of the Ostrogoths, was too much occupied by his quarrel with the Greek Emperor to take advantage of the death of Clovis. Under these circumstances the Franks, so far from losing ground, were enabled to extend the limits of their empire and more firmly to establish their supremacy.

The power of Theoderic the Great prevented Clovis from completing the conquest of Burgundy, and its rulers regained before his death a virtual independence of the Franks. The sons of Clovis only wanted a favourable opportunity for finishing the work which their father had begun, and for changing the merely nominal subjection of Burgundy into absolute dependence. And here again it was internal dissension which prepared the way for the admission of the foreign enemy.

Gundobald, King of Burgundy, died in 517 (A.D.), leaving two sons, Sigismund and Godomar, as joint successors to his throne. The former of these had married Ostrogotha, a daughter of Theodoric the Great, by whom he had one son, Sigeric.

On the death of Ostrogotha, Sigismund took as his second wife a person of low and even menial condition, who pursued the son of the former queen with all the hatred popularly ascribed to step-mothers.

Gregory of Tours relates that the boy increased the bitterness of her feelings against him by reproaching her for appearing on some solemn occasion in the robe and ornaments of his high-born mother. The new queen sought to revenge herself by exciting the jealousy of her husband against his son. She secretly accused Sigeric of engaging in a plot to obtain the crown for himself and represented him as having been moved to this dangerous and unnatural enterprise by the hopes he cherished of receiving aid from his mighty grandfather. This last suggestion found but too ready an entrance into the heart of Sigismund, and so completely poisoned for the time its natural springs, that he ordered Sigeric to be put to death. Inevitable remorse came quickly, yet too late, and the wretched king-buried himself in the monastery of St. Maurice, and sought to atone for his fearful crime by saying masses day and night for the soul of his murdered son.

In the meantime Clothildis, the widow of Clovis, herself a Burgundian princess, who had lived in retirement at the church of St. Martin since her husband's death, did all in her power to rouse her sons to take vengeance on her cousin Sigismund.

It is difficult to conjecture the source of the feeling which thus disturbed her holy meditations in the cloisters of St. Martin's, and filled her heart with schemes of revenge and bloodshed. We can hardly attribute her excitement on this occasion to a keen sense of the cruelty and injustice which Sigeric had suffered. The wife of Clovis must have been too well inured to treachery and blood to be greatly moved by the murder of her second cousin. Some writers have found sufficient explanation of her conduct in the fact that her own father and mother had been put to death in 492 (A.D.) by Gundobald, the father of Sigismund. But we know that when Gundobald was defeated by Clovis he obtained easy terms, nor was the murder of Clothildis parents brought against him on that occasion. It is not likely that a thirst for vengeance which such an injury might naturally excite, after remaining unslaked in the heart of Clothildis for nearly thirty years, should have revived with increased intensity on account of a murder committed by one of the hated race upon his own kinsman. A more probable motive is suggested by a passage in Gregory of Tours, in which he informs us that Theoderic of Metz had married Suavegotta a daughter of Sigismund of Burgundy.

Theoderic, as we have said, was the eldest son of Clovis, by an unknown mother, and was evidently the most warlike and powerful of the four Frankish kings. A union between her stepson and the Burgundian dynasty might seem to Clothildis to threaten the welfare and safety of her own sons, to whom her summons to arms appears to have been most particularly addressed. Theoderic took no part in the present war; and on a subsequent occasion, when invited by Clodomir to join him in an expedition against the Burgundians, he positively refused.

The sons of Clothildis, happy in being able to obey their mother's wishes in a manner so gratifying to their own inclinations, made a combined attack upon Burgundy in 523 (A.D.) Sigismund and Godomar his brother, were defeated, and the former, having been given up to the conquerors by his own followers, was carried prisoner to Orleans; the latter escaped and assumed the reins of government in Burgundy.

The Franks, like all barbarians of that age, found it more easy to conquer a province than to keep it. In the very same year, on the retreat of the Frankish army, Godomar was able to retake all the towns which had been surrendered to the Franks, and to possess himself of his late brother's kingdom.

Clodomir renewed the invasion in the following year. Before his departure he determined to put the captive Sigismund, with his wife and children, to death; nor could the bold intercession of the Abbot Avitus, who threatened him with a like calamity, deter him from his bloody purpose. His answer to the abbot is highly naive. "It seems to me" he said, "a foolish piece of advice to leave some enemies at home while I am marching against others, so that, with the former in the rear and the latter in front, I may rush between the two wedges of my enemies. Victory will be better and more easily obtained by separating one from the other."

In accordance with this better plan, he caused his captives to be put to death at Columna near Orleans, and thrown into a well.

After thus securing "his rear," he marched against the Burgundians. In the battle which took place on the plain of Veferonce near Yienne, Clodomir was deceived by a feigned retreat of the Burgundian army, and, having been carried in the impetuosity of his pursuit into the midst of the enemy, he was recognized by the royal length of his hair and slain on the field of battle.

The loss of their leader, however, instead of causing a panic among the Franks, inspired them with irresistible fury; they quickly routed the Burgundians, and, after devastating their country with indiscriminate slaughter, compelled them once more to submission.

Yet it was not until after a third invasion that Burgundy was finally reduced to the condition of a Frankish province, and even then it retained its own laws and customs ; the only marks of subjection consisting in an annual tribute and the liability to serve the Frankish king in his wars.

On the death of Clodomir, his territories were divided among the three remaining kings; and Clotaire, the youngest of them, married the widowed queen Guntheuca. The children of Clodomir, being still young, appear to have been taken no notice of in the partition: they found an asylum with their grandmother Clothildis.

While his half-brothers were enlarging the Frankish frontier towards the south-east, Theoderic, who had declined to join in the attack upon Burgundy, was directing his attention towards Thuringia, which he ultimately added to the kingdom of Austrasia. The accession of the Thuringians to the Frankish Empire was the more important because they inhabited those ancient seats from which the Franks themselves had gone forth to the conquest of Gaul, and because it served to give additional strength to the Austrasian kingdom, in which the German element prevailed.

The fall of Thuringia is traced by the historian to the ungovernable passions of one of the female sex, which plays so prominent a part in the history of these times.

About 528 (A.D.), this kingdom was governed by three princes, Baderic, Hermenfried and Berthar, the second of whom had the high honour, as it was naturally considered, of espousing Amalaberg, the niece of Theoderic the Great. The "happy Thuringia," however, derived anything but advantage from the "inestimable treasure" which, according to her uncle's account of her, it acquired in the Ostrogothic princess.

This lady was not unconscious of the dignity she derived from her august relative, and fretted within the narrow limits of the fraction of a petty kingdom. Gregory tells us a singular story of the manner in which she marked her contempt of the possessions of her husband, and at the same time betrayed her ambitious desires.

On returning home one day to a banquet, Hermenfried observed that a part of the table had no cloth upon it; and when he inquired of the queen the reason of this unusual state of things, she told him that it became a king who was despoiled of the centre of his kingdom to have the middle of his table bare. Excited by the suggestions of his queen, Hermenfried determined to destroy his brothers, and made secret overtures to Theoderic of Austrasia, to whom he promised a portion of his expected acquisitions on condition of receiving aid. Theoderic gladly consented, and, in conjunction with Hermenfried, defeated and slew both Baderic and Berthar (Werther). A man who, to serve his ambition, had not shrunk from a double fratricide, was not likely to be very scrupulous in observing his engagements to a mere ally. He entirely forgot his promise to Theoderic and kept the whole of Thuringia to himself. He relied for impunity on his connection with the royal house of the

Ostrogoths, his alliance with the Heruli and Warni, and the great increase of his strength in Thuringia itself. But with all these advantages he was no match for Theoderic of Austrasia and his warlike subjects. The death of the latter's great namesake removed the only obstacle which had prevented the Franks from attacking Thuringia. In 530 (A.D.) the Austrasian king summoned his warlike subjects to march against Hermenfried; and, in order to make the ground of quarrel as general as possible, he expatiated to them on some imaginary cruelties committed by the Thuringians upon their countrymen. "Revenge," said he, "I pray you, both the injury done to me, and the death of your own fathers; remembering that the Thuringians formerly fell with violence upon our ancestors, and inflicted many evils upon them, when they had given hostages and were desirous of making peace; but the Thuringians destroyed these hostages in various ways, and having invaded the territory of our forefathers, robbed them of all their property, hung up young men by the sinews of their legs, and destroyed more than 200 maidens by a most cruel death." The enumeration of all these horrors ends with some degree of bathos: "But now Hermenfried has cheated me of what he promised."

The Franks, who required no very powerful oratory to induce them to undertake an expedition in which there was prospect of plunder, unanimously declared for war; and Theoderic, in company with his son Theudebert and his brother Clotaire of Soissons, marched into Thuringia. The inhabitants endeavoured to protect themselves from the superior cavalry of the invaders by a stratagem similar to that employed by Robert Bruce at Bannockburn, by digging small holes in front of their own line.

They were, however, compelled to retreat to the river Unstrut in Saxon Prussia, where they made a stand, but were defeated with immense carnage, so that the river "was choked with dead bodies, which served as a bridge for the invaders." The whole country was quickly reduced and permanently incorporated with Austrasia. And thus, after a long interval, the Franks repossessed themselves of the ancient homes of their tribe, and by one great victory established themselves in the very heart of Germany, which the Komans from the same quarter had often, but vainly, endeavoured to do.

The growing separation between the German and Romance elements in the Frankish Empire, as represented by Theoderic, King of Metz, on the one side, and his half-brother, on the other, becomes more and more evident as our history proceeds. While the sons of Clothildis were associated in almost every undertaking, Theoderic frequently stood aloof, in a manner which shows that his connection with them was by no means of the same kind as theirs with each other. The conquest of the purely German Thuringia, was undertaken by Theoderic exclusively on his own account and in reliance on his own resources. Clotaire indeed accompanied him in his expedition against that country, but in all probability without any military force, nor does he appear to have put in any claim to a share of the conquered territory.

The subjugation of Burgundy, on the other hand, in which the Romance language and manners had acquired the ascendancy, was the work of Clotaire and Childebert alone. Theoderic was invited to join them, but refused on the ground of his connection with the King of Burgundy. Whatever may have been his reason for declining so tempting an invitation, it was certainly not want of support from his subjects, for we are told that they were highly irritated by his refusal, and mutinously declared that they would march without him. Yet he adhered to his determination not to join his brothers, and pacified the wrath of his soldiers by leading them against the Arverni, in whose country they committed the most frightful ravages, undismayed by several astounding miracles!

An inroad had been previously made upon the Arverni, by Childebert, while Theoderic was still in Thuringia. Childebert had suddenly broken off from the prosecution of this war, and turned his arms against Amalaric, King of the Visigoths, who still retained a portion of Southern Gaul. This monarch had married Clothildis, a daughter of Clovis, from motives of interest and dread of the Frankish power; but appears to have thrown aside his fears, and with them his conciliating policy, on the death of his great father-in-law.

We are told that Clothildis suffered the greatest indignities at the hands of Amalaric and his Arian subjects for her faithful adherence to the Catholic Church.

Where religious predilections are concerned, it is necessary to receive the accounts of the dealings between the Franks and their Arian neighbours with the utmost caution. Few will believe that the object of Childebert's march Avas solely to avenge his sister's wrongs; but the mention of them by the historian seems to indicate that the invasion was made in reliance upon Catholic support among the subjects of Amalaric himself. The sudden resolution of Childebert (taken probably on the receipt of important intelligence from the country of the Visigoths), the rapid progress and almost uniform success of the Franks, all point to the same conclusion, that the Catholic party in Southern Gaul was in secret understanding with the invaders. Amalaric was defeated and slain in the first encounter, and the whole of his Gallic possessions, with the exception of Septimania, was incorporated without further resistance with the Frankish Empire. The Visigoths, with their wives and children, retired into Spain under their new king Theudis.

Theoderic, King of Austrasia, died in 534 (A.D.), after having added largely to the Frankish dominions, and was succeeded by his son Theudebert. An attempt on the part of his uncles Childebert and Clotaire to deprive him of his kingdom and his life was frustrated by the fidelity of his Austrasian subjects. How venial and almost natural such a conspiracy appeared in that age, even to him who was to have been the victim of it, may be inferred from the fact that Theudebert and Childebert became soon afterwards close friends and allies. The latter, having no children, adopted his nephew, whose life he had so lately sought, as the heir to his dominions, and loaded him with the richest presents. In 537 (A.D.) these two princes made a combined attack upon Clotaire, who was only saved from destruction by the intercession of his mother. That pious princess passed a whole night in prayer at the sepulchre of St. Martin, and Gregory tells us that the result of her devotions — a miraculous shower of enormous hail-stones — brought his cruel kinsmen to reason!

The Empire of the Franks was soon after extended in a direction in which they had hitherto found an insurmountable barrier to their progress. On the death of Theoderic the Great, or, as he is called in song and legend,

"Dietrich of Bern," the sceptre which he had borne with such grace and vigour passed into the hands of an infant and a woman. The young and beautiful Amalasuintha, daughter of Theoderic by the sister of Clovis, and widow of Eutharic, exercised the royal authority in the name of her son Athalaric; and when the latter, prematurely exhausted by vicious habits, followed his mighty grandfather to the grave in 532 (A.D.), she made Theodatus, son of Amalafrida, the sister of Theoderic, her associate in the royal power. The benefit was basely repaid.

Theodatus procured the murder of the unhappy queen to whom lie owed his advancement, and thus drew down upon himself and his country the vengeance of all who were desirous of dismembering the Empire of the Ostrogoths. Religious animosities, which it had been the policy of the Arian but tolerant

Theoderic to sooth by the even-handed justice of his administration, broke forth with destructive fury under his feeble successors. The Roman subjects of Theoderic's empire had not lost the pride, although they had degenerated from the valour, of their ancestors, and had never ceased to think it shame and sin to be ruled by a barbarian monarch, and that monarch, too, a heretic. They would gladly have consented to forget their former jealousies, and to unite themselves with the Eastern Empire, especially when a temporary gleam of life was thrown over its corrupt and dying frame by the vigorous administration of Justinian. But, if it were the will of Heaven that they should yield to a new and more vigorous race, they wished at least to have an orthodox master, who would not merely protect their religious freedom, but agree with their theological opinions. Their choice therefore lay between Justinian and the Franks, who were ever watching their opportunity to turn the errors and divisions of their neighbours to their own account. Justinian was the first to move; and, under the pretext of avenging the death of Amalasuintha, he sent his celebrated general Belisarius to attack Theodatus. The Franks beheld with joy the approaching struggle between their two mightiest rivals, and prepared to take the advantageous position of umpires.

Both Justinian and Theodatus were aware that the Franks could turn the scale in favour of either party, and both made the greatest efforts to conciliate their aid. Justinian appealed to their natural enmity against heretics and Goths, but deemed it necessary to quicken their national and theological antipathies by a large present of money, and still larger promises. The Franks received the money and promised the desired assistance the more readily, as they felt themselves aggrieved by the murder of a niece of Clovis.

Theodatus, on the other hand, hearing that Belisarius was already on his way to Sicily, endeavoured to ward off the attack of the Franks by offering them the Gothic possessions in Gaul and 2000 pounds' weight of gold. The Franks were dazzled by the splendour of the bribe, but Theodatus died before the bargain was completed. His general Vitisges, who was elected to succeed him, called a council of the chiefs of the Ostrogothic nation, and was strongly urged by them to fulfil the promises of Theodatus, and by sacrificing a portion of the empire to secure the rest.

"In all other respects" they said, "we are well prepared; but the Franks, our ancient enemies, are an obstacle in our path." The imminent peril in which Vitisges stood rendered the sacrifice inevitable, and the whole of the Ostrogothic possessions in Gaul which lay between the Rhone, the Alps, and the Mediterranean, as well as that part of Rhaetia which

Theoderic the Great had given to the Alemanni after their defeat by Clovis, were transferred in full sovereignty to the Franks. The Merovingian kings, regardless of their former promises to Justinian, divided the land and money among themselves and promised their venal but efficient support to the king of Italy. They stipulated, however, out of delicacy to the Greek Emperor, that they should not march in person against Belisarius, but should be allowed to send the subject Burgundians, or at all events to permit them to go. This seasonable reinforcement enabled the Ostrogoths to sack and plunder Milan, in which exploit they received the willing assistance of the Burgundians. In the following year, 539

(A.D.), Theudebert himself, excited perhaps by the alluring accounts he had heard of the booty taken by his subjects in Italy, marched across the Alps at the head of 100,000 men. Vitisges and his Goths had every reason to suppose that Theudebert came to succour them, but Belisarius on his part hoped much from the long feud between Goth and Frank.

Theudebert determined in his own way to be impartial. He had promised to aid both parties, and he had promised to make war on both; and he kept his word by attacking both, driving them from the field of battle, and plundering their camps with the greatest impartiality. A letter of remonstrance from Belisarius would probably have had little weight in inducing Theudebert to return, as he did soon afterwards, had it not been backed by the murmurs of the Franks themselves, who were suffering from an insufficient supply of food, and had lost nearly one third of their numbers by dysentery.

Though our principal attention will be directed to the actions of the Austrasian king, we may briefly refer in this place to a hostile incursion into Spain, made by Childebert and Clotaire, in 542 (A.D.). On this occasion the town of Saragossa is represented by Gregory of Tours as having been taken, not by the sword and battle-axe of the Franks, but by the holy tunic of St. Vincentius, borne by an army of women, clothed in black mantles, with their hair dishevelled and sprinkled with penitential ashes. The heretical Goths no sooner caught sight of the tunic, and heard the first notes of the holy hymns which were sung by the female besiegers, than they fled in terror from their city, and left it to be plundered by the advancing Franks.

As the object of this invasion was simply predatory, the Franks soon after retired into Gaul with immense booty, and the Goths resumed possession of their devastated country.

While Italy was distracted by war, and with difficulty defending itself from the attacks of Belisarius, Theudebert took possession of several towns which bordered upon Burgundy and Rhastia. Bucelinus, the Duke of Alemannia, avIio fought in the army of Theudebert, is said by Gregory to have conquered "Lesser Italy," by which he no doubt meant Liguria and Venetia. These provinces were added to the Frankish dominions, the Ostrogoths only retaining Brescia and Verona.

The cession of territory made to the Franks by Vitisges as described above, was ratified by the Emperor Justinian: and, as a further proof of the growing influence of the Merovingian kings, we may state, that in 540 (A.D.) they presided at the games which were celebrated in the circus of Aries, and caused coins of gold to be struck, bearing their own image instead of that of the Roman emperor.

It is about this period that the Bavarians first become known in history as tributaries of the Franks; but at what time they became so is matter of dispute.

From the previous silence of the annalists respecting this people, we may perhaps infer that both they and the Suabians remained independent until the fall of the Ostrogothic Empire in Italy. The Gothic dominions were bounded on the north by Rhsetia and Noricum; and between these countries and the Thuringians, who lived still further to the north, was the country of the Bavarians and Suabians. Thuringia had long been possessed by the Franks, Rhsetia was ceded by Vitisges, King of Italy, and Venetia was conquered by

Theudebert. The Bavarians were therefore, at this period, almost entirely surrounded by the Frankish territories, in which position, considering the relative strength of either party, and the aggressive and unscrupulous spirit of the stronger, it was not possible that the weaker should preserve its independence. Whenever they may have first submitted to the yoke, it is certain that at the time of Theudebert's death, or shortly after that event, both Bavarians and Suabians (or Alemannians), had become subjects of the Merovingian kings. And thus, in the middle of the sixth century, and only sixty years from the time when Clovis sallied forth from his petty principality to attack Syagrius, the Frankish kingdom attained to its utmost territorial greatness, and was bounded by the Pyrenees and the Alps on the southland on the north by the Saxons, more impassable than either.

Theudebert died in 547 (A.D.), and was succeeded by his son Theodebald, a sickly and weak-spirited boy, of whose brief and inglorious reign there is little to relate. He died in 553 (A.D.), of some disease inherent in his constitution, leaving no children behind him. 2 His kingdom therefore reverted to his great uncles Childebert and Clotaire, the former of whom was a feeble and childless old man, while the latter, to use the language of Agathias, "had only contracted his first wrinkles," and was blessed with four high-spirited and warlike sons.

Under these circumstances, Clotaire considered it safe to claim the whole of his deceased nephew's kingdom; and declared that it was useless to divide it with Childebert, whose own possessions must shortly fall to himself and his sons. To strengthen his claims still further, he married Vultetrada, the widow of Theodebald and daughter of Wacho, king of the Longobards. For some reason or other (but hardly from their objection to polygamy, since Clotaire had actually had at least five wives, not all of whom could be dead), the Christian bishops strongly opposed this marriage. It is not improbable that the fear of false doctrine may have influenced them more than the dread of immorality, and that their opposition in this case, as in many subsequent ones, was founded upon the fact that the new queen belonged to an Arian family.

In the same year in which Theodebald died, Clotaire, King of Soissons, was involved in serious hostilities with the Saxons, the only German tribe whom the Franks could neither conquer nor overawe.

In 555 (A.D.), when forced into a battle with the Saxons at Deutz, by the overweening confidence of his followers, who even threatened him with death in case of noncompliance, he received a decisive and bloody defeat, and the Saxons freed themselves from a small tribute, which they had hitherto paid to the Austrasians.

The kindred Merovingians never lost an opportunity of injuring one another, and Childebert, taking advantage of his brother's distress, not only urged on the Saxons to repeat their incursions, but harboured and made common cause with Chramnus, the rebellious and exiled son of Clotaire. The war which was thus begun, continued till the death of Childebert in 558 (A.D.), when Clotaire took immediate possession of the kingdom of Paris.

Chramnus, having lost his powerful ally, was obliged to submit, and appears to have been in some sort forgiven. In a short time, however, he revolted again, and fled for refuge to Chonober, Count of the Britons, who, since their voluntary submission to Clovis, had remained in a state of semi-dependence on the Franks. Chonober received him with open arms, and raised an army to support his cause, forgetful, or regardless, of the obedience which he nominally owed to the Frankish king. Conscious of his inability to meet Clotaire in the open field, he proposed to Chramnus that they should attack his father in the night.

To this, however, the rebellious son, half repentant perhaps, "virtute Dei prceventus" would by no means consent. Chonober had gone too far to recede, even had he wished to do so, and on the following morning the two armies engaged.

Clotaire, though cruel and licentious, even for a Merovingian, was evidently a favourite of Gregory of Tours, who represents him as marching to meet his son like another David against another Absalom. "Look down," he prayed, "Lord, from heaven, and judge my cause, for I am undeservedly suffering wrong at the hands of my son; pass the same judgment as of old between Absalom and his father David." "Therefore" continues the historian, "when the armies met, the Count of the Britons turned and fled, and was killed upon the field of battle." Chramnus had prepared vessels to escape by sea; but in the delay occasioned by his desire to save his family he was overtaken by the troops of Clotaire, and, by his father's orders, was burned alive with wife and children.

The perusal of that part of Gregory's great work, from which we are now quoting, affords us another curious insight into the condition of the Christian Church in an age which some are found to look back to as one of peculiar purity and zeal. The historian has related to us in full and precise terms the several enormities of which Clotaire was guilty; how he slew with his own hand the children of his brother, in the presence of the weeping Clothildis, and under circumstances of peculiar atrocity; how he forced the wives of murdered kings into a hateful alliance with himself; how he not only put his own son to a cruel death, but extended his infernal malice to the latter's unoffending wife and children. And yet the learned, and, as we have reason to believe, exemplary bishop of the Christian Church, in the very same chapter in which he relates the death of Chramnus, represents the monster as having gained a victory by the special aid of God ! In the following chapter, he also relates to us the manner in which Clotaire made his peace with heaven before his death.

www.ingramcontent.com/pod-product-compliance
Lightning Source LLC
Chambersburg PA
CBHW031403040426
42444CB00005B/397